JIMI HENDRIX

REBECCA POOLE

In Consultation with Martha Cosgrove,
M.A. and Reading Specialist

JUST THE FACTS BIOGRAPHIES

LERNER PUBLICATIONS COMPANY / MINNEAPOLIS

Martha Cosgrove has a master's degree from the University of Minnesota in secondary education, with an emphasis on developmental and remedial reading. She is licensed in 7–12 English and language arts, developmental reading, and remedial reading. She has had several works published, and she gives numerous state and national presentations in her areas of expertise.

Lerner Publications Company
A division of Lerner Publishing Group
241 First Avenue North
Minneapolis, Minnesota 55401 U.S.A.

Website address: www.lernerbooks.com

Library of Congress Cataloging-in-Publication Data

Poole, Rebecca
Jimi Hendrix / by Rebecca Poole
p. cm. – (Just the facts biographies)
Includes bibliographical references, discography, and index.
ISBN-13: 978-0-8225-3532-4 (lib. bdg. : alk. paper)
ISBN-10: 0-8225-3532-7 (lib. bdg. : alk. paper)
1. Hendrix, Jimi–Juvenile literature. 2. Rock musicians–United States–Biography–Juvenile literature. I. Title. II. Series.
ML3930.H45M37 2006
787.87'166'092–dc22 2005017323

Manufactured in the United States of America
1 2 3 4 5 6 - BP - 11 10 09 08 07 06

Contents

CHAPTER 1

First Steps

Before he had a guitar, ten-year-old Jimi Hendrix imagined he had one. He danced around with the kitchen broom. When his father, Al, asked what he was doing with the broom, Jimi said that he was learning to play it. He carried it with him everywhere. When he took it to school, everyone thought he was crazy.

Jimi wanted a real guitar. But Al couldn't afford one. One day, Al found an old instrument called a ukulele, which he gave his son. The ukulele had only one string, but it was better than a broom. Even with just one string, Jimi could actually play some songs on it. It was one of the earliest signs of the talent that would one day make Jimi one of the greatest rock guitarists of all time.

Childhood Changes

Jimi was raised to be quiet. "My dad was very strict . . . . I couldn't speak unless I was spoken to first," he said. Even into adulthood, Jimi was always described as quiet, soft-spoken, and shy. A troubled family life added to Jimi's quietness.

In 1942, Al Hendrix married Lucille Jeter, just before he left to fight in World War II (1939–1945). Before the war, Al and Lucille had been dance partners. They spent their nights in dance halls, ballrooms, and nightclubs. They were great dancers and liked being the center of attention. It was a life that Lucille loved.

Soon after Al left, Lucille found out that she was going to have their baby. Jimi was born in Seattle, Washington, on November 27, 1942. Al was still away at war. Lucille named her son Johnny Allen Hendrix. Because of a mix-up with the U.S. Army, she received no money from Al for nearly a year.

During this time, she and Jimi lived with anyone who would take them in. They moved around a lot and sometimes stayed in very poor conditions.

Eventually, Lucille grew tired of caring for young Jimi. She left him with her mother, other relatives, and friends. She went back to the nightlife she'd enjoyed before Al had gone away. Lucille showed up to see Jimi from time to time. Sometimes she had been drinking before the visit. When friends in Berkeley, California, offered to care for Jimi, Lucille's mother agreed.

When Al got out of the army, he went straight to Berkeley to get his son. He brought the boy back to Seattle. Three-year-old Jimi had never seen the man who was taking him away. Probably even more confusing, Al changed his son's name to James Marshall Hendrix and called him Jimi.

Lucille and Al got back together sometimes. In 1948, they had a second son, named Leon. But their marriage wasn't happy. Lucille often went away for days. The couple often argued. Jimi learned to cope by keeping quiet and getting out of the way. "My mother and father used to fall out a lot, and I always had to be ready to go tippy-toeing off to [my grandmother's]." The couple divorced in 1951.

In 1940, the population of Seattle, Washington, was 368,000. By 1950, it had grown to 465,000.

After the divorce, Lucille still visited her sons. But she had a habit of making promises she did not keep. When Jimi asked his father why she did this, Al told him that Lucille meant well. Jimi and Leon weren't supposed to go to see their mother by themselves, but sometimes they did. Leon later said that she would give them lots of love for a few days. Then she would disappear.

Al had a hard time raising two boys alone and making ends meet. He had no special skills and very little education. He was also African

American. At the time, jobs could be hard for African Americans to get and keep. Al took whatever jobs came up. Finally, he went into business as a yard worker. But work wasn't steady. By moving from place to place, Al and his boys stayed one step ahead of rent collectors.

Jimi attended several Seattle schools, including Leschi Elementary. His best subject there was art. When the teacher told the class to paint something, he painted space battles and fantastic landscapes of other worlds.

At Leschi, Jimi made his only close childhood friend, James Williams. Other children picked on James. Jimi became his defender. The boys helped each other along in a city where most people were white and had plenty of money. They were embarrassed that they

IT'S A FACT!

Jimi Hendrix and James Williams had nicknames for each other. Jimi's was Henry (for Hendrix) and James' was Potato Chips, which is what James always ate. The boys joined the Cub Scouts together. Jimi's father recalled that they were both kicked out of Cub Scouts because they practiced setting fires in the local park.

were poor. They had to wear old or handmade clothes. "Everybody used to laugh at me when I went to school, you know, the regular sob story," Jimi said.

In 1957, when Jimi was fifteen, Lucille went into a hospital with problems related to alcoholism. Al refused to bring the boys to see her. But an aunt went to visit her and brought Jimi along. Jimi stared at Lucille throughout the visit but, as usual, said very little. She died a short time later. Jimi and Leon asked to go to her funeral. Again, Al refused.

Jimi always remembered Lucille fondly. To Jimi, she was a gentle, wandering spirit. Years later, he said that she came to him in dreams and inspired some of his lyrics and music.

A Real Guitar

Around this same time, Jimi paid five dollars for a used acoustic guitar (a guitar that doesn't need an electric amplifier). Jimi was left-handed. The guitar was made for someone who was right-handed. Jimi didn't let that bother him. He turned the guitar upside down and reversed the strings. He quickly learned how to tune the guitar.

Jimi listened over and over to his father's records of great African American blues musicians. It was a relaxed sort of music that relied heavily on the guitar. In the early 1950s, most African Americans listened only to African American musicians. Most whites listened only to music performed by whites. Seattle's radio stations played the music of white musicians. Jimi tuned in anyway and learned all the popular songs. One radio program that he liked was the *Grand Ol' Opry,*

Music and Race in the 1950s

In the 1950s, racism and the segregation (separation) of whites and blacks were part of the U.S. music scene. Many teenagers, both white and African American, enjoyed rock and roll. White people often regarded this style as African American music. Racist whites didn't want white teenagers mixing with African American teens or performers. Racism stopped many white and African American musicians from performing together. Similarly, dancing between whites and blacks was usually prohibited.

Dick Clark hosted a popular TV dance show called *American Bandstand.* He waited until 1958 to have an African American dance couple on his show because he was scared of public criticism. Around the same time, Alan Freed was fired from his new television show after he featured a young black performer dancing with a young white woman. Radio stations and record stores whose customers were mostly white people often refused to carry albums by African American musicians.

which featured some of the greatest guitar players of the time.

He took his guitar everywhere, practicing constantly. The guitar became his voice. With his guitar, the shy Jimi Hendrix could speak out. At first, he played for his father. But soon, he played for anyone else who would listen. Al found a new respect for his son as he watched him struggle to master the guitar. He saw that the guitar was to Jimi what dancing had been to him in his own youth.

By the time Jimi got to Garfield High School, he had grown to be a tall boy with long arms and very large hands. He was still shy but was becoming interested in girls. And when he found

When Jimi was a junior at Garfield High School, his picture appeared in the school yearbook.

that music attracted them, his interest in music grew. James Williams was left to fend for himself. From that point on, Jimi's best friend was his guitar.

Jimi's First Band

In 1959, Al bought Jimi his first electric guitar, a white Supro Ozark. Jimi and some other boys from Garfield High formed a band, the Rocking Kings. One of the members had an amplifier. The amp cranks up the volume of an electric guitar. The band's first paying job, or gig, was at the National Armory in Kent, Washington. The Rocking Kings each earned thirty-five cents for their show.

It's a Fact!

Jimi never learned to read or write music. But he listened carefully to songs and, by trial and error, played them on his guitar. In the process, he discovered what he could make the instrument do.

The pay was always low, but the Rocking Kings began to get gigs in and around Seattle. Like most pop groups of the time, the Rocking Kings dressed alike and moved to carefully planned steps on stage. They played rock and roll and rhythm and blues (R&B) hits with a solid beat.

When he wasn't playing with the Rocking Kings, Jimi went to the Seattle nightclubs. He listened to African American musicians as well as white musicians. He tried to learn from both styles.

Jimi's skill grew quickly. He began experimenting with the amp, looking for ways to make sounds that were his own. He told the other members of his band that he thought a guitar could sound like a horn. They laughed at him. He once decorated his guitar with feathers. The other band members lectured him. Sometimes he'd break into unplanned solos onstage. He was playing differently and better than anyone else. The band was jealous of him. Soon the Rocking Kings drifted apart, but Jimi kept playing wherever he could.

As performing became more important to Jimi, school became less important. Jimi's nightlife began to include running around with friends. Sometimes he got into trouble. He and a buddy broke into a store and stole some clothes, which they later gave to a charity. Twice, he went joyriding with friends in a stolen car. He got caught both times, and the events were recorded on his police record. In 1959, his senior year at Garfield High, he dropped out of school.

Jimi had no high school diploma. He had car theft charges on his record. Jimi would have a tough time earning a living. Briefly, he went to work for Al as a laborer. But he needed something more steady. He joined the U.S. Army to become a paratrooper. He'd learn to parachute from planes. The step pleased his father, but for Jimi, it was a risk. Jimi was someone who always believed in doing his own thing. That kind of thinking would not go over well in the military.

In the Army

Jimi stood at the open door of the aircraft and threw himself into the sky for the first time. Afterward, he wrote home to Al from Fort Campbell, Kentucky. He described that first parachute jump with the U.S. Army's 101st Airborne Division as "outta sight." He told of the sound of the airplane's roaring engines and of the air rushing by as he fell toward the earth.

Years later, in an interview, Jimi described how he felt when he jumped. "It's the most alone feeling in the world . . . you're scared [the parachute] won't

Jimi completed his army basic training at Fort Hood, California, in 1961. Then he joined the 101st Airborne Division at Fort Campbell, Kentucky.

open. . . . Then you feel that tug on your collar and there's that big beautiful white mushroom above you."

Back in the barracks, where the soldiers slept, Jimi tried to reproduce on his guitar the sounds and emotions he had experienced in the jumps. He named his guitar Betty Jean and started talking to it. Then he began taking it to bed with him. Keeping Betty Jean close by made sense in the barracks, where things could get stolen. But the other men found his actions strange. They started hiding his guitar and bullying him. Once, some of them even beat him up.

Although he felt like an outsider, Jimi had two friends at Fort Campbell. One was Raymond Ross, the heavyweight boxing champion for the 101st Airborne. Ross had known Jimi in Seattle, and he stood up for his friend. Because Ross was so tough, nobody bullied Jimi anymore.

Jimi's other friend was Billy Cox, a fellow enlisted man. Billy had studied classical music as well as the blues and R&B. When Billy heard Jimi play the guitar, he knew Jimi had special talent. Billy introduced himself and said that he could play the bass guitar.

Billy and Jimi formed an R&B band called the King Kasuals. In their free time, they played at the clubs on and near the base. In spite of the strict military life, music had come back into Jimi's life.

Jimi said later that he'd hated army life from the start. Nevertheless, he earned his Screaming Eagle patch. This is the symbol that members of the 101st Airborne wear on their uniforms. He completed twenty-five successful jumps with the paratroopers but broke his ankle on the next jump. Because of the injury, Private First Class James Hendrix left the military on July 2, 1962.

Chapter 2 Following a Dream

FORT CAMPBELL WASN'T FAR from Nashville, Tennessee, home of the Grand Ol' Opry. Nashville was known for its guitar greats and hopefuls. After leaving the army, Jimi stayed near the base. He was waiting for Billy Cox, who was also going to leave. Together, they'd head for Nashville. At the age of 20, Jimi was about to begin the life of a professional musician.

***(Above)* the Grand Ol' Opry occupied the Ryman Auditorium in Nashville, Tennessee, when Jimi was there.**

Finding a Sound

Jimi had already been influenced by a lot of music. His father's recordings of Charlie Christian and T-Bone Walker taught him valuable playing techniques. These included bending or vibrating the guitar's strings to create jazz and blues sounds. Jimi also liked the joyous music of the African American churches he'd attended with relatives. The services were filled with music, movement, and energy. He liked the music of Elvis Presley. He saw the first African American musicians "cross over" into the white pop music scene. Little Richard created "Tutti-Frutti," and Chuck Berry scored with "Maybellene." But it was the great African American blues guitarist Muddy Waters who had the greatest effect on Jimi. He never forgot the rough, forceful sound of Waters's amplified guitar.

It's a Fact!

The blues is a form of music that African American musicians created in the early 1900s. The blues have a slow, sad sound. This style can be sung or just played on an instrument without any singing.

In Nashville, Jimi and Billy found that the paying gigs were hard to find.

MUDDY WATERS

Born in Mississippi in 1915, Muddy Waters *(below)* first picked up a guitar at the age of seventeen. He soon became skilled at the intense, raw, painful music that reflected the harsh life for African Americans in the South. He also mastered the use of a "bottleneck" on the strings of the guitar. This technique helped the guitar notes slip and slide with the vocals. He also had learned to control his powerful voice. By 1943, Waters had moved to Chicago, Illinois. He held other jobs while he tried to make a name for himself as a blues guitarist. Slowly, his career took off, and he started recording with some of the great blues musicians of the time. During his career, he became known as the "father of Chicago blues." He died in 1983.

The city had many talented musicians. The competition was stiff. Jimi later said that there was no need to go to a club to see a good guitar player. They were everywhere, even sitting out on their front porches.

When he was broke, Jimi sometimes slept in the streets. He pawned (sold) his guitar when necessary. Even when he had a guitar, he could not always afford new strings. One night, he was playing without an E string. A young bass guitarist named Larry Lee gave him one. Larry began hanging around with Jimi and Billy.

Learning the Ropes

Jimi quickly learned that to survive in Nashville, a musician needed a stage show. It wasn't enough to play the guitar well. Everybody in Nashville could do that. Jimi needed to use his whole body to get the audience's attention. Even in Seattle, Jimi had experimented with dramatic stage movements. When he'd been with the Rocking Kings, he had tried playing the guitar behind his head and between his legs. The audience had liked it. By the time he left Nashville, he was playing the guitar with his teeth as a way to get the audience's attention.

In 1963, at the age of twenty-one, Jimi began touring with other African American performers. They played in bars, restaurants, and clubs throughout the United States. Jimi backed up many famous musicians, including Sam Cooke, Jackie Wilson, the Supremes, and Little Richard. As a backup, he played their music the way they wanted. He was used to the wandering life and knew the rules–keep moving and don't get attached to people. He switched bands often. But regardless of how often he switched or the miles he traveled, Jimi was playing the same music over and over. Bored and frustrated, he returned to Nashville.

On the way to Tennessee, he stopped in Chicago to visit Chess Records. This company is the recording home of many famous African American blues performers. Jimi hung around the studios. He was hoping to get invited into a recording session. By chance, Muddy Waters walked in, and Jimi got a free lesson on the blues. When played right, Waters said, the blues were almost a religious experience.

Jimi continued on to Nashville. He knew he wasn't going to improve musically by being a backup. He was working toward his own unique musical style. He needed to find a place where that style could develop and be heard. Jimi must have thought that place might be New York City. Before he left Nashville, Jimi told Larry Lee that he had some songs and was heading north. He didn't have a coat, so Larry gave him one. In fact, except for his dreams, Jimi had very little.

Struggling in New York

In 1964, when Jimi got to New York City, he went straight to the African American district of Harlem. Located at the northern tip of Manhattan, Harlem has a history of both glory and misery. During the 1920s, famous African American writers and poets lived there. Harlem was a center for jazz musicians. Theaters and nightclubs, such as the Apollo Theater and the Cotton Club, gave many entertainers their start.

But Harlem declined rapidly after the Great Depression hit in 1929. The district became one of the United States's poorest ghettos. People living there had few opportunities and little hope. By the time Jimi arrived in Harlem, civil unrest was at an all-time high. Many Americans–both black and white–were working hard to fight against racism. But some African Americans were growing angry because change just never seemed to come. This anger soon erupted into riots. The violence made life in the ghettos even worse.

Jimi failed to find a paying gig in Harlem. He was hanging out at a nightclub where musicians jammed (played for fun) late into the night. One evening, he met Fay Pridgeon, a woman who had personal contacts with many Harlem musicians. Fay saw something special in the young guitarist. She took Jimi home and fed him. Soon they moved in together. Usually broke, they skipped from one cheap hotel to the next to

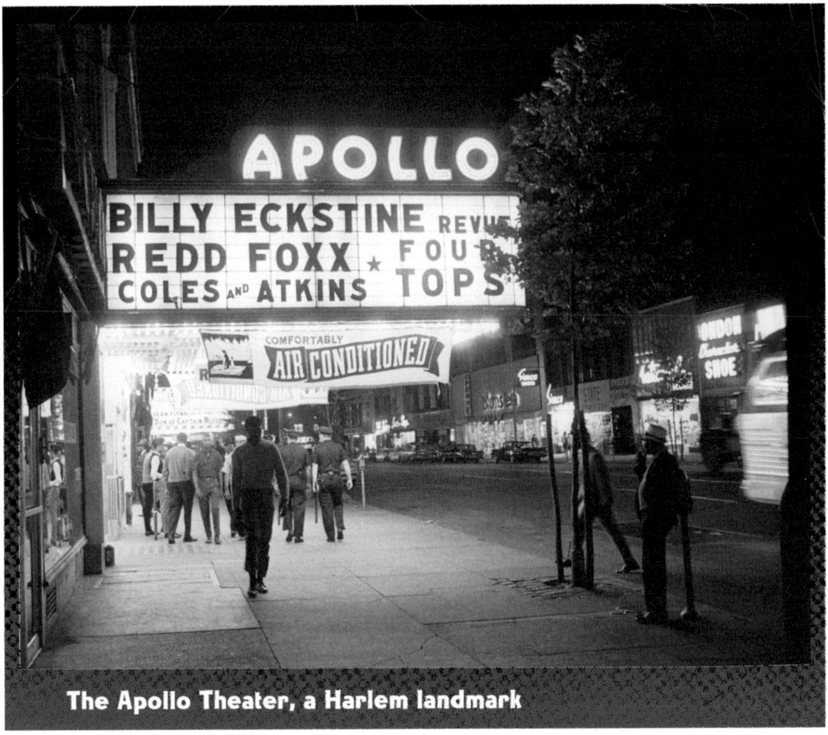

The Apollo Theater, a Harlem landmark

avoid paying their rent. They slept most of the day and listened to blues records for hours. At night, they went to the clubs. This lifestyle was like the life Jimi's mother, Lucille, had loved.

To get money, Jimi pawned his guitar again. Fay asked other musicians to lend him one in case he was invited to jam. He rarely got to perform. But when he did, the audience liked him. Through her connections, Fay got Jimi a chance to play on amateur night at the Apollo Theatre.

IT'S A FACT!

The Apollo's amateur night launched the careers of many talented performers. These musicians included Ella Fitzgerald, Michael Jackson, Lauryn Hill, James Brown, and D'Angelo.

MAKING CONNECTIONS

Years earlier, many of the Apollo's amateur-night winners had gone on to become stars. The same chances were unlikely by the mid-1960s. But there was still a $25 prize, money that Jimi and Fay could put to good use. Of course, to win, the amateur had to impress the very tough Apollo audience. The audience didn't just boo the performers they disliked. They threw bottles or even furniture at entertainers who failed to please. If the audience insisted, the host of the show shot the performer with a fake gun. Anyone who stepped onto the stage of the Apollo had better be good.

Jimi was up to the challenge that night. He walked away with the $25 prize and went right back to looking for gigs in the local clubs. Finally, a scout for the Isley Brothers, a successful R&B and soul group, heard Jimi play. The Isleys hired Jimi to make a record with them and then go on tour.

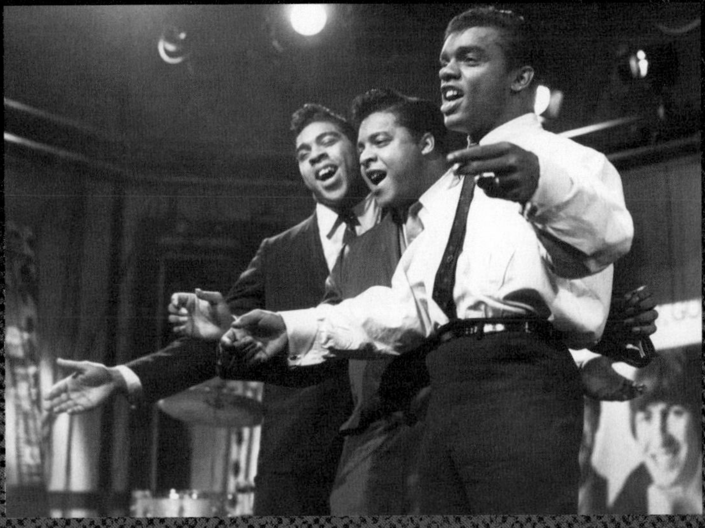

Jimi worked with the Isley Brothers *(above)*. He played for their performances and recording sessions.

Unlike other groups, the Isley Brothers let Jimi add a little of his own style into the performances. He got to dazzle the audience with his solos. When Jimi's guitar was stolen, the Isley Brothers bought him his first Fender guitar, a Duo-Sonic. For the next nine months, Jimi recorded, lived, and toured

Jimi's Guitars

Very few left-handed guitar models were available to Jimi Hendrix, a left-handed player. Instead, Hendrix would flip the guitar over and restring it. One advantage to this idea was that the volume and the tone controls were easier to adjust because they were now at the top of the guitar.

Jimi Hendrix's guitar of choice was the Fender Stratocaster. Hendrix once said, "The Stratocaster is the best all-around guitar for the stuff we're doing. You can get the very bright trebles and the deep bass sound." Jimi received his first Fender guitar in 1964. It was a blond Duo-Sonic. He soon traded that guitar for his first Stratocaster.

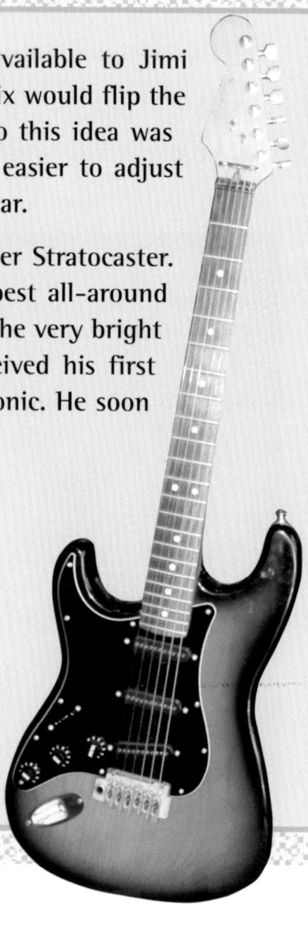

A left-handed Fender Stratocaster electric guitar

with the Isleys. Yet the band said they never really got to know him. He was so focused on his guitar that he sometimes let it do his talking. When one of the other band members asked him a question, Jimi would answer by striking a note on the guitar.

It wasn't long before Jimi got restless again. He left the Isleys and went back on the road with Little Richard. But Richard didn't like competition. When Jimi and another band member started showing up in frilly shirts and wild colors, Richard told them to stop. Only one person on that stage was going to look pretty, and it was going to be Little Richard.

Jimi quit Little Richard's band and joined a couple of other groups. But he again decided that he'd had enough of traveling as a backup musician. He liked hearing the top 40 R&B songs, but he didn't like playing them every night.

Jimi went back to Harlem and Fay. In a letter to Al, he said that he was doing okay, although he didn't eat every day. Despite his lack of money, Jimi was still hearing the music around him. He spent his last few dollars on Bob Dylan's new album, *Highway 61 Revisited.* Jimi played the album over and over. Fay could never understand what he heard in it. But the poet in Jimi responded to

Bob Dylan's voice and songs influenced Jimi's music.

Dylan's serious lyrics and unique voice. Some say that it was the influence of *Highway 61 Revisited* that drew Jimi away from Harlem. He left Fay and went to Greenwich Village. The clubs in this part of New York had mainly white audiences.

Greenwich

Greenwich Village had art galleries, theaters, and popular nightclubs. Broke again and without a guitar, Jimi took a job playing backup for Curtis Knight and the Squires at the Cheetah. This club was the village's hippest nightspot. The Squires played standard blues, soul, and rock hits. They soon found that the more Jimi played, the bigger the audience grew. Curtis gave Jimi some spending money. He also lent Jimi a guitar and gave him a little freedom on stage.

Curtis's producer, Ed Chalpin, offered Jimi a three-year recording contract with his company, PPX. The deal wasn't good for Jimi. Under the contract, he couldn't legally work for other recording companies for three years. The contract gave him only a 1 percent royalty (payment) on any profits made from his writing, playing, or producing. He got only a $1.00 bonus for signing the contract. Jimi had never made big money performing, so he signed. Why fight for a bigger share of nothing?

Jimi played with the Squires until he could buy a guitar. Then he started his own band. He called it Jimmy James and the Blue Flames. Gigs were hard to find. The band often had no money and no place to live. Jimi later recalled the life of a jobless musician: "We even tried to eat orange peels and tomato paste. Sleeping outside those tall [buildings]. . . . Rats running all across your chest, cockroaches stealing your last candy bar."

The Hendrix Sound

Jimi's way of playing the guitar was unique. He used electronic noises, such as the feedback of the amps or the sound of a breaking guitar. He did whatever he could to make these noises. He often vibrated the strings and adjusted the control dials on both the guitar and the amps for new sounds. Even his body position could make a difference in how his guitar sounded.

Eventually, Jimi and his band played clubs such as the Café Wha? and the Café Au Go Go. They got the attention of visiting musicians, including Paul Butterfield, a blues harmonica player. Butterfield described Jimi's sound as "jets taking off . . . nuclear explosions, and buildings collapsing . . . B-bb-bbb-room! He was just mowing me down." Jimi was already creating all the musical sounds he would use during his career. He was playing with only an electric guitar and some simple equipment.

A Big Break

Linda Keith, the girlfriend of guitarist Keith Richards of the Rolling Stones, saw Jimi perform one night. She stepped in to help him. She had good connections in the music business. Linda told

Jimi to sing during his performances. But Jimi had always been shy about his singing voice. Linda asked the Stones's producer to watch Jimi perform. She wasn't discouraged when the producer said Jimi was too wild. Linda thought Jimi just needed direction and a break. She saw a conflict in him between his love for playing the blues and his desire to be a rock star.

Linda also knew Chas Chandler. He was the bass player for the British rock group the Animals. Like other popular British bands, the Animals had based their music on American blues. The band was in New York and about to break up. Linda heard that Chandler was looking for a new career as a record producer. She asked him to come to Café Wha? where Jimi was playing.

Jimi played at Café Wha? in New York's Greenwich Village.

That night, Jimi performed "Hey Joe." Chandler loved it and wanted to produce the song. He was amazed at what Jimi could do. Jimi was able to use his guitar in new ways. He could make the instrument give him different sounds at the same time. Chandler had never seen another guitarist with that ability. Chandler had found the act he was looking for.

In 1965, Chandler asked Jimi to move to Britain and work for him, Jimi had only two questions. Could he meet Eric Clapton, one of

Eric Clapton in the 1960s

Britain's top blues guitarists? And were the British amps any good? Chandler assured him on both points. Jimi stuffed all his belongings—including his guitar—into his guitar case and took off to meet new audiences. Little did he know that these audiences would be more suited to his style. His days of sharing candy bars with cockroaches were over.

IT'S A FACT!

Jimi didn't tell his father about going to London. In fact, most of his friends didn't know he was leaving. When Jimi arrived in London, Chas introduced him to the London music scene quickly. One of the places he first visited was the Scotch of St. James. The Scotch was an expensive nightclub that musicians, actors, models, and other young, hip people went to in the 1960s.

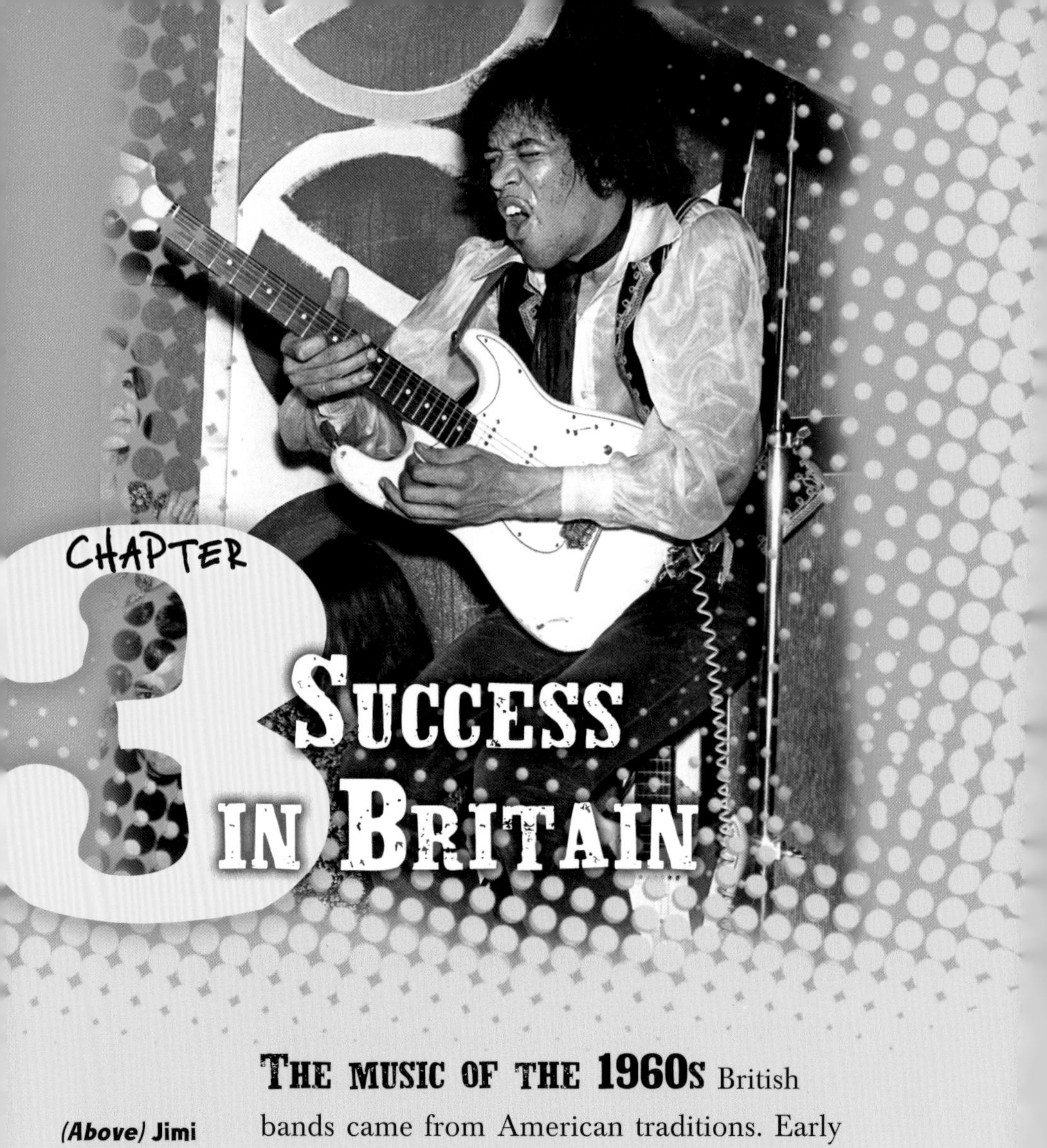

CHAPTER 3 SUCCESS IN BRITAIN

(Above) **Jimi had been ignored in the United States. But he was a star in Britain.**

THE MUSIC OF THE 1960S British bands came from American traditions. Early hits by the Beatles were straight out of American rock and roll and R&B. The Who had music based on R&B. The Rolling Stones and the Animals added American blues to the mix. Britain's best rock guitarists struggled for a sound that grew from these traditions. They heard that sound in September 1966, when a twenty-four-year-old Jimi Hendrix hit the music scene in London, Britain's capital.

The sounds coming from Jimi's guitar stunned London's leading rock musicians. Everyone wondered why Jimi hadn't been a hit in the United States. Musicians wanted to hear Jimi and learn.

Chas Chandler quickly got Jimi started. Within hours of arriving in London, Jimi was jamming with other musicians. He met a woman named Kathy Etchingham. He was immediately attracted to her.

Jimi relaxes with Kathy Etchingham.

Jimi had many female admirers, but Kathy was different. He felt something deeper for her. She set up an apartment for Jimi, and they lived together during his stay in London.

Building a Band

Chandler got Jimi gigs in the clubs where powerful people in the music industry gathered. A singer named Johnny Hallyday asked Jimi to join him on tour the next month. Jimi needed to find a band fast. Mostly by chance, he and Chandler chose Noel Redding and Mitch Mitchell.

Redding had played as a backup musician for years. He'd become discouraged by his lack of success as a guitar player. Like Jimi, he'd never made much money in the business. He'd come to London one last time to look for work with a band. But Redding had never before played bass guitar, the instrument he would play in the new band. That wasn't a problem for Jimi, though. He liked that Redding wouldn't have any set ideas about what a bass guitar could do. Jimi also liked Redding's afro (puffy) hairdo, so he hired him.

Mitchell was a skillful drummer who was working as a session musician. Session musicians work in recording studios but aren't part of any band. Mitchell was growing bored with this life, so he tried out for Jimi's band. Despite stiff competition, Mitchell got the job.

Swinging London

In the 1960s, British music—from groups such as the Beatles *(below),* the Rolling Stones, and the Who—poured into the United States. London, the capital of Britain, became the center of cultural and social changes that were aimed at art, writing, fashion, film, as well as music. The term "Swinging London" described the feeling at the time. Young people in their late teens and early twenties flocked to London nightclubs, such as the Scotch. New and modern clothing—such as miniskirts and bell-bottomed pants—became the norm. Colors in art and clothing were loud and bright. Plays and films explored new themes. The films that feature the fictional superspy Austin Powers are a playful way to remember Swinging London.

Jimi's band was set. They just needed a name. Chandler thought that the name Jimi was going by–Jimmy James–wasn't quite right. Jimi Hendrix was a better fit. The band's name, The Jimi Hendrix Experience (JHE), was a group decision.

Next, the JHE had to put together a show. They had three days before the tour began, and

The Jimi Hendrix Experience: ***left to right,*** **Mitch Mitchell, Jimi Hendrix, and Noel Redding**

they had no original material. They would have to play their own versions of soul and R&B songs that Jimi and Redding knew from their years as backup guitarists. Jimi communicated with his band mates musically–not verbally. He taught them songs by playing the music and letting them learn it by ear. According to Redding, Jimi gave them "the basic chord structure and tempo within a framework . . . we each found our own parts, and a song and an arrangement would emerge." Mitchell enjoyed the freedom that Jimi's style allowed.

The band still had one major problem–nobody wanted to sing. Since Jimi was the only band member with a good voice, he would have to be the lead vocalist. Jimi wasn't happy about singing. At first, he was so nervous that he drowned out his singing by turning up the volume of the music. But soon, he gained enough confidence to let his voice be heard. Still, Jimi never became really comfortable singing in front of others.

IT'S A FACT!

Jimi often sat behind the sound equipment so the other musicians could not look at him while he sang.

The band also had many equipment problems. Jimi pounded his guitars hard. They quickly went out of tune. Jimi always had the volume on his amps set at full blast. The amps constantly had to be repaired or replaced. The volume made hearing each other nearly impossible. On their first gig, Mitchell couldn't hear at all. He had to watch the guitarists' hands and hope he guessed right about the timing. Later, Mitchell bought four huge speakers to help with this problem, but even that was not a perfect solution.

IT'S A FACT!

Jimi always had his amps on full blast. Musicians call this the Hendrix setting.

MONEY MATTERS

While the musicians hurried to get their act together, Chandler was busy with other things. His choice of Mike Jeffery as comanager of the JHE was interesting. He had managed Chandler's old band, the Animals. He was known for his messy bookkeeping. The band members all were fairly sure he had cheated them. Still, Jeffery was great at making deals, handling contracts, and setting up tours. He took over most of the band's business dealings. Chandler worked on the creative and production tasks.

For tax reasons, Jimi was to be paid as an employee of Jeffery's company, Yameta. Chandler and Jeffery were also paid through Yameta. Together, the managers received 40 percent of the JHE's profits. Even for the music business, this was a lot of money. Mitchell and Redding were paid a weekly salary. They also got a small royalty on concerts and record sales.

Jeffery did not always pay the band as planned. Sometimes he paid in cash. Other times, Jimi and his band mates got bank deposits. They never really knew how much they'd earned. Most likely, they were paid only a small portion of what the band actually took in. None of the three musicians knew much about money.

Of course, it did take money to get a band started. Chandler and Jeffery had to buy back all the contracts Jimi had signed in New York. (They missed only one–the PPX contract.) They also had to support Jimi until he got settled in London. The managers also had to pay for publicity and equipment costs. The band didn't make a profit for more than a year. Chandler may have even sold some of his own guitars to pay expenses.

The tour with Hallyday gave the band experience working together. Jimi also had time to work on his stage show. He had learned that he needed to be fun to watch to get the audience excited. Jimi's stage show included squatting down, diving to the floor, and rolling around. He even wagged his tongue in time with the beat and bit the strings of his guitar. His style was wildly physical. This experience both frightened and thrilled the audience. Even Mitchell was scared the first time he saw Jimi perform.

Hey Joe

To survive, the band needed a hit song. The band went to a recording studio to make a record of "Hey Joe." Jimi still wasn't confident in his songwriting skills. He wanted to use another established song as the flip (back) side of the record. Chandler changed his mind, though. He said that it was time for Jimi to show his talent as a songwriter. In December, three months after

Jimi's arrival in Britain, the single was released. The song Jimi wrote for the flip side was called "Stone Free."

While they waited to see if "Hey Joe" would succeed, the JHE began a short tour of Germany. During one of these performances, Jimi accidentally discovered how guitar busting added to the show. An excited fan pulled Jimi off the stage. As he climbed back up, he threw his guitar ahead of him. The guitar was damaged, its strings broken. Jimi later told an interviewer that he hadn't meant to damage the guitar at first. But since it was already broken, he finished it off by smashing it. The electronic screeching from the amp and the violence of the act itself were pure Hendrix. It wowed the audience and made the headlines. Guitar busting became a part of the act.

When he got back to Britain, Jimi tried to contact his father. Excited about his career, he telephoned Al at 1:00 A.M., Seattle time. Al didn't like being woken up at that hour. He spoke harshly to his son. A short time later, however, Jimi and Al had another phone conversation that went better.

Shock Rock

Shock rock has become its own style of music. Jimi was not the only musician to grab the media's attention with onstage actions. Performers use props, costumes, fireworks, and other things to produce an exciting show. Alice Cooper, GWAR, Marilyn Manson, Ozzy Osbourne, and KISS are among shock rock stars.

Jimi damaged a lot of guitars during his career.

Meanwhile, Jimi's managers continued to build his image. Knowing that it would make the band famous, they encouraged Jimi's wild behavior on stage. Jimi went along with the idea. According to Chandler, he and Jimi looked for new ways to offend the right people. They wanted to make sure that the JHE ended up in the headlines. Soon the press was referring to Jimi as the Wild Man of Borneo, and the band was being advertised with such names as the New Weirdo Trio.

Jimi's wild image was his ticket to the stardom that he had wanted. Soon he would realize that once he became a star, his image could also be a trap that was hard to escape.

Chapter 4 Free Falling

(Above) Jimi's talent placed him firmly at the top of Britain's music scene in 1967.

JIMI'S SECOND SINGLE was called "Purple Haze." According to Chas Chandler, Jimi wrote the song while waiting to go onstage. Chandler and Jimi worked on the sound in the recording studio until they got the effects they wanted. Unlike "Hey Joe," this song showed

Jimi's originality, both as a songwriter and a performer. The song on the flip side, "51st Anniversary," was also original.

Jimi was pleased with the unique sound of "Purple Haze." Electronic equipment and new ways of recording music had opened up new creative directions. The lyrics of both songs also kept the public and press buzzing. They wondered what Jimi's lyrics meant. He wrote about a spell that caused him to "kiss the sky." Was that spell love or drugs? Others said the lyrics came from a dream or a Native American myth. Jimi explained the lyrics differently every time he was asked.

Things started to happen quickly for the JHE in the spring of 1967. "Hey Joe" had moved up the pop music charts (the list of the most popular songs) to number 4. The

IT'S A FACT!

Music charts are polls that let the public know which album or CD, single song, or musician is the most successful during that week or month. Charts are advertising for the musicians. Music companies use music charts to help promote and sell their products.

group appeared on British television and started a tour. During this tour, Jimi ended one of the shows by burning his guitar. The stunt got everyone's attention. Theater managers threatened to ban the band. But many young people couldn't wait to see what Jimi would do next.

Back in London, the band had a great show at the Saville Theater. Other famous rock musicians praised the band. Nicknames like Mr.

The JHE's growing fame led to appearances on British television.

Phenomenon began to pop up in the press's descriptions of Jimi. "Purple Haze" was released in March and moved to number 3 on the music charts. Still, some people said the band played noise, not music. Despite the critics, the JHE was growing more popular. At the age of twenty-four, Jimi was a star. The next two years would be a frenzy of interviews, events, concert tours, and recording sessions.

Jimi was glad to be a success. But he also knew that the public expected a certain sound from him. He wasn't ready to give up his creative freedom. Word spread about Jimi's crazy behavior onstage. People expected him to do more outrageous things. But Jimi still cared more about the music. He still wanted to make a name for himself beyond "Purple Haze."

In a very early interview, Jimi said he'd like his music to be called free feeling. It was a mixture that he had been developing over his entire lifetime. He wanted it to keep growing and changing. Jimi made his point when he released his third single, "The Wind Cries Mary." The song wasn't like his earlier releases. It was a gentle ballad. He had written it after a fight with Kathy Etchingham, whose middle name was Mary. The single may have surprised Jimi's fans, but it still rose up the charts to number 6.

Experience

Shortly after "The Wind Cries Mary," the JHE released its first album, *Are You Experienced?* In recording it, Jimi worked for the first time with sound engineer Eddie Kramer. Kramer was able to understand and mix–or blend–the sounds just as Jimi imagined them. From that point on, Kramer was a big influence on Jimi's recordings.

Together with Chandler and Kramer, Jimi experimented with the effects he could get out of the recording-studio equipment. These included playing music backward, using varying speeds, and other distortions. Kramer's mixing skill allowed different instruments and sounds to be stressed (easier to hear). His skill also kept Jimi from having to play the tracks over and over for the right recording. That kept Chandler happy, since studio time was expensive.

Jimi and Kramer used feedback–squealing noises from a microphone–as part of the music. The result, *Are You Experienced?* was not only exciting but impossible to place in any one musical category.

Jimi's own term, "free feeling," is a good way to describe the album. Every song is different. "Red House," for example, is Jimi's tribute to the American blues. In "Manic Depression," Jimi describes his hopelessness of loving a woman. He contrasts those feelings to the sweet reliability of music. The song has a unique beat that almost makes it seem like music for a waltz (a formal kind of dance).

The ballad "May This Be Love" suggests the image of a waterfall in a green forest. It is an example of what Jimi called his sound paintings.

Mixing Music

In the early days of recording, a band had to perform a song repeatedly until all the parts sounded exactly the way they wanted them to sound on a record. Then came multitrack recording. In this style, one track—or sound element, such as the singing or the drums—was recorded at a time. This allowed the musicians to focus on problem areas and rerecord only the parts that needed fixing. Mixing allowed recording engineers to add, remove, or stress sounds. Musicians could move around sections of a song. They could combine sounds in different ways on the same song and decide what version they liked best. They could even take away sounds that no longer worked. These techniques sped up recording sessions because musicians no longer had to play their songs over and over again. And since most musicians rented the recording studio's time, less time meant less money spent on making the record.

These attempts to create a musical image went on throughout his career. In "Third Stone from the Sun," Jimi re-creates through sound the outer-space landscapes he painted in elementary school.

The title song, "Are You Experienced?" explains how to listen to Jimi's music. Its lyrics tell listeners to experience the music with Jimi, not to just hear it. He asks listeners to "cross over" to a place where they can accept the free form of his music. Most music experts agree that *Are You Experienced?* was one of the most important first albums in the history of rock.

Jimi already saw how easy it was to lose that free feeling in both his music and his life. Fans bought his records and paid to see him perform. But they also expected to see the image–not the person. They wanted to hear the hits the way they'd heard them before. This frustrated Jimi. During a concert in May 1967, he struggled to tune his guitar properly. The crowd got impatient. They weren't worried about the quality of the music. They just wanted the show to start. In a fit of anger, Jimi snapped the strings off his guitar. He then trashed his amps, which blew out all of the lights.

But this was no time to stop on the road to fame. Mike Jeffery had gotten the band a U.S. recording contract with Warner Brothers. *Are You Experienced?* was shooting up the charts. The band was also invited to perform at a huge rock concert to be held a month later in California. How could any musician who'd ever pawned his guitar say no?

MONTEREY

By 1967, popular music had gone through some big changes. Both sound and lyrics were growing deeper. Jimi's music was a big part of this change. His experiments with the electric guitar brought new sounds into popular music. People started to change the way they thought about rock and roll. In June, the Beatles released *Sgt. Pepper's Lonely Hearts Club Band*, one of the most famous albums in rock history. *Sgt. Pepper* had a variety of musical styles and strange electronic effects. It inspired many other musicians. That summer, California's Monterey Pop Festival was held. This huge outdoor rock concert became the perfect gathering place for musicians and fans experimenting with personal and creative freedom.

1960s Music Scene

American teenagers were heavily drawn to the British rock-and-roll music of the early 1960s. By the late 1960s, however, the music scene in Britain was changing. Offshoots, such as psychedelic rock and hard rock, were developing. Groups such as the Yardbirds became hard rock acts, as their music became more energetic and gritty. Other bands such as Cream and Pink Floyd *(below)* were termed psychedelic bands, because they experimented with bizarre sounds and drug-inspired images.

The Monterey Pop Festival took place at a time when many young people were unhappy with the direction the United States was taking. They protested against the unpopular Vietnam War (1957–1975). Tension between black and white Americans had started riots. At the same time, street drugs such as marijuana and LSD became easier to get. Many people who experimented with these drugs had no idea of how destructive they could be.

Rock groups like Jefferson Airplane and the Grateful Dead were featured at the Monterey show. Their songs often encouraged drug use. But Monterey wasn't just about these sorts of bands. It also featured straight pop, R&B, and soul acts. A few bands from Britain were scheduled–the Animals (who had started playing again), the Who, and the JHE. Jimi and his band fit in well with the musical lineup.

IT'S A FACT!

Jimi performed at the Monterey Pop Festival held in Monterey, California, in 1967. Musicians played for free, and all the money went to charity. Thirty-one bands showed up, including the Jefferson Airplane, The Mamas and the Papas, the Steve Miller Band, Simon and Garfunkel, Janis Joplin, and the Grateful Dead.

The Who and the JHE were both hoping a good performance would increase their popularity in the United States. Both groups liked to finish their shows by destroying equipment, so neither band wanted to go after the other. Each band wanted the chance to be the first to shock the audience.

Behind the stage, Jimi got into an argument with the Who's Pete Townshend. Each man argued that his band should go first. When Townshend said his band should start, Jimi stood on a chair and started to play his guitar. Townshend later said that the message Jimi was sending was "Don't mess with me!" The men finally agreed to a coin toss. Jimi lost the toss.

The Grateful Dead came on after the Who, which had left broken bits of equipment all over the stage. Next, Brian Jones (a member of the Rolling Stones) introduced the JHE. Jimi put everything he had into this performance. He came onstage wearing a pink feather boa. He began hammering the audience with "Killing Floor" and "Foxy Lady." He followed this with an exciting performance of Bob Dylan's "Like a Rolling Stone." He played the solo parts first with his teeth, then behind his head. He ended the show with "Wild Thing," using every trick he had, including somersaults. In a final salute, he set his guitar on fire, smashed it into pieces, and threw the bits to a screaming audience. Jimi's return to the United States had been a success.

Jimi sometimes played his guitar with his teeth. The audience in Monterey liked this trick.

After the show, the JHE went to a party in Laurel Canyon, a suburb of Los Angeles. The party included music and drugs. Jimi had used drugs before, but his use really increased after Monterey. The band spent days playing jam sessions and taking LSD. During this time, Jimi met a woman named Devon Wilson. The two were attracted to each other. They liked to party and do drugs together.

The JHE had come to the United States with only the single Monterey booking and a weeklong gig at San Francisco's Fillmore West Auditorium. They succeeded in thrilling their California audiences. They even bumped Jefferson Airplane from top billing at the Fillmore. But, in general, the U.S. media were unimpressed with the band. *Billboard*, which covers the music and entertainment industry, described their concerts as more show than music.

Fillmore West and East

Beginning in the early 1960s, a rock-and-roll promoter named Bill Graham brought groups to the Fillmore West in San Francisco. This club became so popular that Graham opened a similar one—the Fillmore East—in New York in 1968. (It closed in 1971.) Groups that regularly performed at the Fillmores included the Jefferson Airplane, the Allman Brothers Band, and the Grateful Dead. The best-known groups often alternated between the two locations. Music groups, including No Doubt, Sonic Youth, and Radiohead, still play at the Fillmore West.

Fillmore owner Bill Graham *(seated right)* was a rock-and-roll promoter. Here he chats with *(left to right)* Paul Kantner and Grace Slick (members of the Jefferson Airplane) and Jerry Garcia of the Grateful Dead.

Touring the United States

Despite the critics, offers came in. Mike Jeffery grabbed them eagerly. He knew that big bucks were to be made in live appearances. First on the list was an offer to appear as the supporting act for a popular band called the Monkees. From Jeffery's point of view, this was a great opportunity. Next to the Beatles, the Monkees were the biggest draw in the United States. Hoping to capitalize on Beatlemania, a TV

The Monkees

company had put together the Monkees. This good-looking group of four young men appeared in a TV program directed toward families and young teens.

Only two of the Monkees were musicians. For the TV show, studio musicians secretly played the instruments. When the Monkees appeared in concert, they pretended to sing to audiences that screamed in appreciation. They were, in fact, very good at what they did. But what they did was very different from what Jimi did. Monkees' fans were young and often came to concerts with their parents. That audience was not ready for Jimi's loud, guitar-smashing act. When the JHE came onstage, some parents stood up and dragged their children away. Many fans booed Jimi and shouted for the Monkees. Others just sat quietly, not knowing what to think. The crowds' reaction depressed Jimi, and he sometimes refused to perform.

Chandler looked for an excuse to get Jimi out of the tour. He told the press that the band hadn't quit. Instead, he said that a women's group called the Daughters of the American Revolution had forced the band off of the tour. Chandler had made up the story, but the press believed it. *Newsweek* and other well-known publications reported the story.

Daughters of the American Revolution

The Daughters of the American Revolution (DAR) was created in 1890. It is a nonprofit group dedicated to education, patriotism, and historic preservation. Its members are the female descendants of patriots who supported American colonists during the American Revolution (1775–1783). To become a member, a woman must prove she is related to a patriot of the war. The DAR is not a political organization, but its members have sometimes taken up political work. At the time of the Monkees tour, the DAR was seen as a white, conservative group that wouldn't approve of Jimi. Chas used this view of the DAR as a way to get Jimi out of the tour.

The JHE stopped in New York City. Jimi visited Fay Pridgeon, his former girlfriend from Harlem. He also jammed with some old music buddies. He sat in on a recording session with his old friend, Curtis Knight. Jimi thought he was simply helping Curtis. He didn't want to be identified as one of the performers. Ed Chalpin, Knight's manager, promised to keep Jimi's name secret. But he later broke that promise. Even worse, he filed lawsuits against other recording companies that had released Jimi's work. He said that Jimi's old PPX contract–the one that his managers had overlooked–was still in effect.

In August of 1967, the U.S. version of *Are You Experienced?* was released. At the same time, the

The Jimi Hendrix Experience did a lot of traveling. The band spent weeks at a time on the road.

band struggled with the tough touring schedule that Jeffery had set up for them. They had money problems. The weeks of touring were wearing down the band members. And audiences came expecting Jimi to jump around the stage and destroy things.

Noel Redding said that the band's drug use was high during the tour. Before a show, they took drugs that helped get them excited. Afterward, they took different drugs to calm them down. They used LSD frequently. Their behavior was getting out of control.

During a flight between tour stops, Jimi wrote the lyrics to his next single release, "Burning of the Midnight Lamp." The song's lyrics are the words of a lonely man, tired of a life that he no longer controlled. When the tour ended, the JHE headed back to Britain. Their tour had gone well musically, but the band was tired.

CHAPTER 5

ROCK ON—AND ON AND ON

JIMI WAS TWENTY-FOUR years old when the JHE returned to Britain in August of 1967. He was there to record his next album, *Axis: Bold as Love.* Jimi worked closely with the studio engineers and technicians. They perfected new sounds suited to each song. Although the result was what some consider the JHE's best work, Jimi felt he had been rushed.

"EXP," the opening song, sends the listener off on a trip full of surprises. The gentle "Little Wing" is followed by the crazy rhythm and heavy rock of "If 6 Was 9." This song sent a message that it's okay to be different. But it was in "Bold as Love," the album's title song, that Jimi finally got the sound he wanted. The song presents colors expressed through music. Each color stands for an emotion. Jimi and Eddie Kramer used a recording technique called phasing. In phasing, swirling sounds seem to come from behind and around the listener in stereo. To Jimi, the recording sounded the way he imagined the song in his head.

Recording time in the studio was expensive. But Jimi only cared about the quality of the album he was making. He said he was willing to spend every cent he had to make it good. Chandler, however, watched the clock nervously as Jimi repeated anything that didn't sound perfect to him.

Problems Build

During this time, Jimi also continued to party. A large crowd of people always followed Jimi into the studio. The crowd included other musicians and fans who wanted to be part of the scene. These people gave Jimi energy. But they also distracted the band from their work. This, in turn, increased the studio hours and expense.

Mitch Mitchell worked hard on the album. He also put up with Jimi's demanding studio behavior. But Noel Redding was bothered by all the repeated tracks, which he considered to be wasted time. Bad feelings soon grew between him and Jimi. Another problem was the band's LSD use. Chandler saw LSD as dangerous. He thought the drug was making Jimi moody and difficult. Jimi may have thought the drug was inspiring him. But some of his lyrics weren't making any sense. Even Redding, a big drug user himself, saw the problem. Drugs were slowing down the recording sessions and helping to destroy everything the band had built together.

Axis was released in Britain on December 1, 1967. Back in the United States, Ed Chalpin had a surprise for Jimi and his management. A few days after *Axis* came out, he released a different album, *Get That Feeling: Jimi Hendrix Plays and Curtis Knight Sings.* This album was made from the Curtis Knight recording session that Jimi had joined with the promise that his name would not be used. Although *Axis* sold well, the unauthorized (not approved by

Chandler *(right)* was furious about the illegal album, *Get That Feeling: Jimi Hendrix Plays and Curtis Knight Sings.* Jimi *(left)* was embarrassed that his name was on an album of such poor quality.

Jimi) Chalpin album actually competed with *Axis*'s sales.

At about this time, the JHE began its second tour of Britain. Jeffery set a tough pace: thirty-two shows in twenty-two days, followed by a series of appearances in Scandinavia. Near the end of this tour, Jimi told an interviewer that if he kept doing the crash-and-burn act the audiences wanted, he'd be dead in two years. He also hinted at wanting to bring other musicians into the band. He said that he was tired of the limits placed on a band with only three members.

On January 3, 1968, Jimi was arrested in Gothenburg, Sweden, for destruction of property. Jimi had smashed everything but the telephone in one of the band's hotel rooms. He told the police that he had been drinking alcohol and couldn't remember anything he'd done. He thought it was possible that someone had mixed a drug in his drink. An alcohol-drug mix may have sparked the explosion. But it was likely that stress, frustration, and being tired played a role as well.

Return to the United States

Jeffery paid little attention to Jimi's problems. He knew that most rock performers make most of their money in their first two years. He didn't want to miss out, so he booked the JHE's next U.S. tour in early 1968. He set up an exhausting schedule for the band. During the first half of the tour, they played in forty cities in fifty days.

The tour included a stop in Seattle. Jimi had not seen his family in nearly seven years. He was nervous about going back and seeing his father. In one of his songs, Jimi wonders out loud what Al would think if he could see how far his son had come. He had always wanted his father's approval. When the JHE played in Seattle, he finally got it.

By 1968, the Seattle landscape had changed since Jimi had lived there.

Jimi had attended Garfield High School in Seattle. He went back for a visit in 1968.

Jimi's visit to his old school, Garfield High, did not go as well. He had been invited to speak at an assembly. There, he was to be given an honorary high school diploma and the keys to the city. It turned out that it was a city holiday, and the diploma and the keys never appeared. Jimi, who expressed himself better in music than speech, was overcome with shyness. After a few words, he hurried away to his limousine.

From this point on, according to Redding, there was no fun left in the life of the band. Like many touring rock groups in those days, the JHE used more drugs when they were on the road. Often, the audiences were also on drugs. They didn't care about the music. They only wanted to see the wild stage show. Some fans stole from the band. Others followed the band everywhere, hoping for any kind of contact. All three band members became nervous. Jimi was the most affected. He became more and more moody. But the band was drawing huge crowds and making a lot of money, most of which went to Chandler and Jeffery. The tour established them as a leading act in rock.

Electric Ladyland

Between gigs, the band recorded at New York City's Record Plant. Eddie Kramer worked there. Jimi was happy to work with his favorite sound engineer again. Jimi wanted more control over the next release, *Electric Ladyland*, which was to be a double album. He wanted to bring in other musicians and instruments for some of the songs. Most of all, he did not want to be rushed.

Jimi had trouble using recording studio time well.

None of this would have mattered to Chandler if Jimi had used his studio time well. But the people Jimi brought in slowed down the process. Jimi was redoing songs over and over. Redding said that Jimi wasn't concentrating. He couldn't get his ideas across to him and Mitchell. Jimi had also become critical of Redding's playing. He often played the bass parts himself.

Chandler began to feel left out of the band's decisions. He knew that Jimi was listening to others now. Some of the people he listened to were making his behavior worse. For example, Devon Wilson had followed Jimi from California. She rented an apartment for him in New York City. Devon was often with Jimi in the studio. She was even in the recording booth, although she had no knowledge of the equipment. Mike Jeffery was also trying to get more control of Jimi. He was involving Jimi in new business deals. Chandler felt that drugs were affecting Jimi's mood and his thinking.

Eventually, Jeffery took over as band manager. He and Jimi started a new company called Are You Experienced? Ltd. Jeffery continued to make the band's deals and also took in 40 percent of the profits. He focused on getting the band back out on the road. Making money at more gigs was of most importance.

Jimi may not have cared how well his records sold, but he did want his music to be heard. That wish was coming true. The 1968 U.S. tour was selling out everywhere the band went. More than a million copies of *Are You Experienced*? had been sold.

Axis was near the top of the charts. But Jimi had lost an important supporter in Chandler. Jeffery was in control, and he cared mainly about profits. Regardless of the personal cost, Jeffery was determined that the band would rock on–and on and on.

CHAPTER 6 CHANGES AND REARRANGES

THE LONG-AWAITED *Electric Ladyland* was almost finished at the end of August 1968. Jimi was pleased with the double album, which was a sort of declaration of independence for him. Its unique guitars and vocals mixed together many musical styles, including blues, R&B, and jazz. Most of the songs represent Jimi's famous style. But a few of them, including, "1983 . . . A Merman I Should Turn to Be" and "Moon, Turn the

***(Above)* Jimi at work in the recording studio**

Tides," surprised his fans with a soothing, magical sound. "Rainy Day, Dream Away" and "Still Raining, Still Dreaming," are laid-back jams with other musicians. Redding and Mitchell did not play on these two songs.

The album also shows some of the emotions behind the music Jimi created. He included "Burning of the Midnight Lamp," a song with lyrics that tell of the darker side of a rock star's life. In "Gypsy Eyes," he sings of a lost love. And in "House Burning Down," he makes a rare statement about politics and racism. Its lyrics question why his fellow African Americans were destroying their own neighborhoods during violent riots.

Riots

Dr. Martin Luther King Jr., along with many others, tried to use peaceful means to stop unfair treatment of African Americans and other minorities. But in spite of their efforts, violent riots sometimes broke out. The first riots took place in Harlem during the summer of 1964. Jimi lived there at the time. The following summer, thirty-four people were killed and nearly nine hundred injured during riots in the Watts section of Los Angeles. Nearly one hundred riots occurred in cities across the country in 1968, after Dr. King was assassinated. Jimi's song, "House Burning Down," expresses his worry about the violence.

Jimi said that he'd delayed the release of *Electric Ladyland* on purpose. He was waiting for the public to be ready for the changes they would hear. He was tired of fans who expected him to get up onstage and do some damage every time he performed. He wanted to change his stage act.

New Directions

During the second part of the 1968 U.S. tour, Jimi became quieter onstage. He concentrated on the music rather than on the stage tricks. During a set of concerts in San Francisco, he invited other musicians to appear with the band. The performances often seemed like the jam sessions he loved. Some fans accepted the changes. Others expected him to at least burn something and screamed at him if he didn't.

Redding said that by this time the band was clearly going downhill. The crew often needed forty-five minutes to talk Jimi into going on stage. He would tell his stage manager to give the fans their money back because he didn't feel like playing.

At the same time, *Electric Ladyland* was climbing in the charts. Touring continued to bring in more and more money. The band was reaching the height of its popularity. But all three members knew that something had changed forever. Jimi told Mitchell and Redding to branch out on their own. He wanted them to find projects separate from the band. The band members decided together that they would alternate between working together in the JHE and doing their own things. They hoped that this plan would give them new energy and ideas. At the start of 1969, the JHE returned to London. Rumors said that the band would break up soon.

In London, Jimi briefly got back together with Kathy Etchingham. He told her about his unhappiness with his career. Etchingham said that Jimi was sick of his image and his stage act. In an interview, he tried to say how serious he was about his music. Jimi called it electric religion.

Music may have been religion to Jimi, but it still meant money to Mike Jeffery. He continued to book the JHE on tours. The band members went along with Jeffery's decisions. It was hard not to, since the JHE had become the highest-paid band performing. Besides, they weren't quite sure yet what else to do. Following some poor performances in Europe, they headed back to the United States to begin what would be their last tour together.

Finding Trouble

Jimi's state of mind was fragile. So was the band's sense of unity. But if they could hold it together, this tour would be the biggest moneymaker ever. They would make more than $1 million. Jeffery added a gig in Toronto, Canada, at the last minute for an extra $110,000. On May 3, 1969, when the band members flew into Canada, they passed through customs (where officials sometimes search people entering a country). Canadian officials

Jimi was serious about his music. He called it electric religion.

arrested Jimi for having a drug called heroin. Was he guilty? Many of his fans thought that he probably was. His drug use was no secret. But most of his friends said that he was not a heroin user. They claimed that the bust was a setup. Jimi himself denied knowing that the drug was in his bag. The charges and the fear of going to prison hung over him for the next eight months.

Jimi ran into trouble again a few weeks later. Jimi played at the Newport Pop Festival in

Jimi *(left front)* talks with backup musicians at the 1969 Newport Pop Festival.

Members of the Black Panthers attend a rally. Formed in 1966, the Black Panthers was a self-defense group. Its goal was to protect African Americans from unfair and brutal police practices.

Devonshire Downs, California. Members of the Black Panthers approached him backstage. The Black Panthers were an African American group that wanted to use violence to win racial equality. They stood against the peaceful civil rights protests of Martin Luther King Jr., who had been killed the previous year. They may have asked Jimi for money or for him to speak out supporting their cause.

Jimi's feelings about race were similar to his feelings about politics. Next to his music, they just didn't seem as important. Jimi thought of himself as a citizen of the world. He hoped to reach people through his music, which stood for freedom and against unfairness.

Still, Jimi knew about the civil rights struggles of the time. He had faced racism growing up. He understood why so many African Americans were angry. He had tried to speak out on behalf of tolerance and nonviolence in his songs. In 1969, he appeared at several benefit concerts for African American causes.

What happened between the Black Panthers and Jimi at the Newport Pop Festival isn't known. But the visit seemed to affect Jimi's performance onstage. He became angry with the crowd when they made noise during the softer songs. He spent much of the time with his back to the audience. Mitchell later described the Newport gig as one of the lowest points in the band's history.

A week later, before he left the stage of the Denver Pop Festival, Jimi made an announcement that surprised his own band. He told the audience that this was the last time the JHE would appear together in concert. Redding, shocked and angry, left the United States. Jimi moved to a rented house in rural New York. A few months later, he explained why he made the decision: "I don't want to be a clown anymore. I don't want to be a 'rock and roll star.'" Jimi had come to a crossroads. Later, in a song called "Earth Blues," he would write about "changes" and "rearranges" that had to be made. For Jimi, the time for those changes had come.

CHAPTER 7

CLOSING ACTS

(*Above*) **Cars and people jam the highway leading to Woodstock.**

THE WOODSTOCK MUSIC and Art Fair spanned a long weekend in August 1969. Called Three Days of Peace and Music, Woodstock was, to many, a fitting end to the 1960s. The decade had been a time of political and cultural confusion. The festival was held on farmland in rural Bethel, New York. On the first day, traffic extended for 20 miles (32 kilometers) along the route to the festival. Hundreds of thousands of people came. They swarmed across private land and over fences.

Festival officials gave up on the idea of charging admission.

Food, water, and bathrooms were in short supply, but drugs and alcohol were not. The festival had a first-aid tent with a nurse, but there was little

Jimi is listed as a performer on the poster advertising Woodstock.

The Birth of Woodstock

In 1969, John Roberts, Joel Rosenman, Michael Lang, and Artie Kornfeld met. Lang and Kornfeld wanted to build a recording studio for rock musicians in the area of Woodstock, New York. But they needed money to pay for it and suggested holding a concert. Roberts and Rosenman had money to invest. Plus they liked the idea of an opening-day concert. It could showcase local talent, as well as draw in more investors and the press. The investors believed a large, three-day concert that was open to the public could pay for the entire studio. Soon the four men were planning what would become the largest concert of the time.

Problems arose nearly from the start. Early publicity showed that large numbers of people were expected. Concerned local citizens forced the planners to find another location. The four rented 300 acres (121 hectares) of a dairy farm in Bethel, New York. Days before the concert even began, floods of people began arriving. The promoters were unable to collect or sell tickets. The concertgoers simply jumped or smashed the fences. Suddenly, the concert had become free of charge. Rosenman and Roberts didn't know if they would be bankrupt. In the end, the entire festival cost about $3.4 million. The investors lost about $100,000. Although the concert didn't make any money, it became a cultural phenomenon.

need for it. Soon it started raining, and everyone was standing in 2 inches (5 centimeters) of mud. Despite these conditions, the festival was mostly peaceful. There were three deaths–one accidental and two drug overdoses–and one birth. And there was music. People who protested the Vietnam War sang alongside Vietnam veterans. Those who supported the government stood with those who opposed it. All types of people were there to enjoy the music.

Some of the biggest names in music were hired to perform. Jimi Hendrix would be the closing act.

Jimi hails the crowd at Woodstock. His performance at the end of the festival would become a symbol of U.S. social and political struggles of the 1960s.

Some of the performers could not get through the traffic jam. This often left long delays in the program. Some musicians refused to go onstage until they were paid in cash.

Since he'd broken up the JHE, Jimi had been living near where the festival was held. He spent the time jamming with friends, many of whom were jazz musicians. At times, he went to a studio in New York City to record material for a new album.

Jimi in the studio

During recording sessions, Jimi surrounded himself with a party atmosphere, which slowed progress. Only his manager and money problems stopped him from going on like this forever.

Mike Jeffery saw Jimi heading away from the moneymaking rock scene. He pressured Jimi to bring back the original JHE–or something like it–as soon as possible. He wanted Jimi to make more rock albums and get back on tour. He wanted Jimi to be making money.

Other pressures were also building. Jimi still owed Ed Chalpin an album from the lawsuit settlement. His new recording studio, Electric Lady Studios, in New York City was costing more than expected. The Canadian drug charge was still hanging over him. Worst of all, he was feeling that he couldn't write

IT'S A FACT!

In the spring of 1968, Warner Brothers settled part of Ed Chalpin's lawsuit against the JHE. Chalpin got royalties from the first three albums the group made. He also got the full rights to a fourth album. In addition, he was allowed to sell recordings that Jimi had made before he became famous.

anymore. He thought all his music was beginning to sound the same.

Taking the Stage

Jimi took the Woodstock gig for a fee of about $30,000. He called on his musician friends for the show. These included Billy Cox, his old army buddy, on bass and Larry Lee, who had given Jimi his coat in Tennessee, on rhythm guitar. He asked Mitch Mitchell to join them on drums. The band seemed more like a family. He named it Gypsy Sun and Rainbows. Together, they went onstage in the early morning of August 18. It was near the end of the Woodstock festival.

Many of the music fans had gone home by the time Gypsy Sun and Rainbows tuned up. Mitchell later recalled that the band didn't come together well. He described the performance as more like a jam session than a concert, "with a lot of stops and starts." But, for many, the highlight of the entire festival came when Jimi played his startling version of the national anthem.

When it is sung, it is easy to forget that "The Star-Spangled Banner" is a song about war. Nobody forgot it this time. With a single guitar, Jimi fired rockets and exploded bombs. Around the anthem's theme, he sent airplanes diving, sirens wailing, and engines screaming. His playing gave the crowd reminders of Vietnam and the civil rights battles being fought in U.S. streets. He added a bit of the song "Taps" to the performance. It's a sad song that

Jimi's performance at Woodstock was recorded and can be seen on the film *Woodstock*.

causes many people to think of death. When asked later why he'd played the national anthem in that way, Jimi said he was responding to the conflict he saw all around him.

After Woodstock

After Woodstock, Jimi started rehearsing regularly with Billy Cox and drummer Buddy Miles. Because both Billy and Buddy were black, some saw this as Jimi's efforts to stop criticism of his own "whiteness." Some saw it as his attempt to come back to black musical traditions, where he had begun. Jimi named this new group the Band of Gypsys. He recorded their live performances at New York's Fillmore East Auditorium as the album he owed Ed Chalpin. Jimi's political side came up again on this album, called *Band of Gypsys,* in the antiwar song "Machine Gun." He dedicated this song to all soldiers who were fighting in U.S. cities, as well as in Vietnam. The album included only six tracks (two by Buddy Miles). It had its high points and sold well, but it was not up to Jimi's standards.

By January 1970, some of the pressure on Jimi was gone. He had been cleared of the drug charges in Canada. He had given Chalpin his album. But he was involved again with Devon Wilson, a drug user. Friends say that he was also using drugs nearly all the time. These included the dangerous drug cocaine. During a New Year's Eve concert with the Band of Gypsys, Jimi simply stopped playing and sat down on the drums. The group tried to keep playing, but Jimi could not go on. He unplugged his guitar and, shivering, left the stage.

Mike Jeffery's response to the miserable performance was to fire Buddy Miles. He asked Redding and Mitchell to re-form the JHE with Jimi. He set up a tour, called the Cry of Love, for them. Jimi was not feeling well enough to tour. His relationship with Redding had been bad since the breakup of the band the year before. But because of money problems, he had to agree.

By April, when the band started its tour in Los Angeles, Jimi had replaced Redding with Billy Cox. He also had some new material, which audiences received politely. The tour was uneven. Jimi canceled some appearances due to illness. But the band put in some very good performances as well.

During a stop in Seattle, Jimi talked with Freddie Mae Gautier, whose mother had helped care for him as a child. He asked her questions about his mother, Lucille. He showed Freddie Mae the lyrics of "Angel," a ballad he had written after his mother had appeared to him in a dream.

Gautier asked Jimi how he was managing his money. He seemed unsure of how much he had or where it was. He told her when he needed money, Mike Jeffery always gave it to him. He also told her that he was trying to get off drugs. He told Gautier that his friends gave him drugs for free. She told Jimi that a real friend wouldn't give him something so harmful.

The recording studio at Electric Lady Studios was ready in June. Around this time, Jimi started to regain control of himself and his musical direction. He began working with sound engineer Eddie Kramer again. Jimi recorded several new songs for a double album, which he was thinking of calling *First Rays of the New Rising Sun.* In some of these songs, he replaced the electronic sounds with instrumental pieces. He also started other projects and was planning to work with several serious jazz musicians.

FINAL DAYS

In an interview in September 1970, Jimi said the era of music begun by the Beatles with *Sgt. Pepper* was over. It was time for something new–and he wanted to be there. "I want a big band full of competent musicians that I can conduct and write for. . . . Music is going to change the world next time." He also said, "Music can [open your mind] . . . you don't need drugs."

With Electric Lady Studios, Jimi became the first major artist to run his own recording studio.

Jimi also made plans to end his contract with Mike Jeffery. But first, he had one more tour to make with the re-formed JHE. He, Cox, and Mitchell headed for the first tour stop on Britain's Isle of Wight. The concert went poorly. The atmosphere was tense from the start. Some of the audience demanded to be let in for free. The band

Fans packed the grounds of the music festival on the Isle of Wight in Britain.

had not rehearsed, and it showed. They had equipment problems. Jimi was also trying some of his new material, which didn't work well onstage with just a trio.

Following a few dates in Scandinavia, the group headed for the German island of Fehmarn. The show was more of a nightmare than a concert. Billy Cox was having emotional problems and could barely perform. In the audience were bands of motorcyclists with guns. Several of the groups were fighting with one another. The band's road manager later remembered that the crew just managed to get the gear packed up before the bikers set the stage on fire.

The JHE returned to London. Cox was sent back to the United States. He had been a good friend to Jimi. As someone who didn't use drugs, he had helped give the group stability. Depressed, Jimi went to see his former manager, Chas Chandler. They talked about how Jimi wanted to go back to working with him and Eddie Kramer. Chandler agreed to listen to tapes of his latest work. Perhaps Jimi wanted to know that he was moving in the right direction with his music and his life.

Late in 1970, Jimi started to reorganize his career.

On September 17, 1970, Jimi called his lawyer. He told him to begin breaking the ties with Mike Jeffery. He spent the day with a girlfriend, Monika Dannemann. He had met her at one of his German concerts in 1968. They went together to her apartment that evening. He had arranged a jam session with Mitchell and another musician later at a club. He never showed up.

Exactly what happened during that night and the following morning is not known. However, a few things are certain. At some point, Jimi took a large (but not normally deadly) dose of Dannemann's sleeping pills. He had also had some alcohol. The combined effect of what Jimi had taken was strong. He vomited but was unable to stop the fluid from going to his lungs and choking him. At the age of twenty-seven, Jimi Hendrix was dead.

Many Questions

Many questions followed the death of Jimi Hendrix. There were even rumors of suicide or murder. An investigation was held in London. Witnesses were called and questioned, but there was simply no way of knowing exactly how and why Jimi had died. Jimi's body was brought back to the United States and was buried in Renton, Washington, near Lucille.

During his lifetime, Jimi authorized the release of only a few albums. These albums represent most of his best work. But many other releases were made before and after his death of which he would not have approved. He left no will, so friends and family fought for years over the control of his lyrics, music, and money. (By 1995, these matters had been sorted out in favor of Jimi's family.)

The remaining members of the JHE continued to create music long after Hendrix's death. Both Mitch Mitchell and Noel Redding wrote books about their experiences with the group. (Redding died in 2003.) Chas Chandler formed a new production company after breaking ties with Jimi. He died of a heart attack in 1997. Devon Wilson died in 1971, after falling from a hotel window. Mike Jeffery was killed in a midair collision during a flight back to London in 1973. And Monika Dannemann, the last person to see Jimi alive, died in 1996 from an apparent suicide.

Monika Dannemann

The tangle of Jimi's personal life did not prevent his music from living on. Jimi inspired many musicians, including blues artists Stevie Ray Vaughan, Robert Cray, and ZZ Top. He also inspired rock guitarists such as Vernon Reid, Eric Clapton, and Lenny Kravitz. His songs have been performed or recorded by rock, jazz, blues, and even classical musicians. His recordings continue to be in demand, as new fans come to appreciate his sound.

IT'S A FACT!

In 1999, Al Hendrix began building a Jimi Hendrix memorial in Renton, Washington. It would be a place for fans to visit. Al died in April of 2002, two months before the memorial was opened.

Jimi never really trusted words. For Hendrix fans, one truth rises above all the words. Jimi was the greatest electric rock guitarist who ever lived. He is in his music. Look for him there.

Glossary

album: a series of recorded music sold together. Albums were originally released on 12-inch phonograph records. Albums later came out on cassette audio tapes and compact disc (CDs).

Grand Ol' Opry: the longest-running musical show on radio. The show features country music and broadcasts from Nashville, Tennessee.

guitar: a popular stringed instrument. Two main types of guitars exist–acoustic and electric. An acoustic guitar is hollow and has a hole in its center. Its sound comes from vibrations as the guitarist strums and plucks the strings. An electric guitar is solid and has a chord that's hooked up to an amplifier. Controls, called pickups, on the guitar change the vibrations of the steel strings into electric current. The current goes into the amp. Pickups can change the sound that comes out of the amp in a lot of ways.

LSD (lysergic acid diethylamide): a major mood-changing drug made from a fungus that grows on cereal grains

paratrooper: a soldier who is trained and equipped to jump out of an airplane

pop music: the short form of popular music. This refers to music that is heard and sold in the popular mass media. Pop music festivals are held throughout the United States.

segregation: the separation of one group of people from another based on race or ethnic background

Source Notes

5 Chris Welch, *Hendrix: A Biography* (New York: Quick Fox, 1978), 12, 15.

6 Ibid., 12.

9 David Henderson, *'Scuse Me While I Kiss the Sky: The Life of Jimi Hendrix* (New York: Bantam, 1983, 1996), 443.

14–15 Harry Shapiro and Caesar Glebbeek, *Electric Gypsy* (New York: St. Martin's Press, 1995), 38.

26 Ibid., 673.

29 Ibid., 103.

30 Charles Shaar Murray, *Crosstown Traffic* (New York: St. Martin's Press, 1990), 42.

56 *Rock & Roll, Volume 4: Plugging In* (Boston, WGBH Educational Foundation and the BBC, 1995).

83 Chris Potash, *The Jimi Hendrix Companion: Three Decades of Commentary* (New York: Simon & Schuster, 1996), 24.

95 Mitch Mitchell, *Jimi Hendrix: Inside the Experience* (New York: St. Martin's Press, 1990), 140.

95 Potash, 36.

Selected Discography

Many of the Jimi Hendrix albums on the market are actually unapproved albums. These albums don't represent his music well. The following is a list of the releases authorized by Jimi, along with a few good releases after his death.

Are You Experienced? (1967; remastered 1993). This outstanding first album introduced Jimi Hendrix's sound. It changed forever the sounds possible from the electric guitar.

Axis: Bold as Love (1967; remastered 1993). This album shows Jimi's growing talents as a guitarist, songwriter, and lyricist.

Electric Ladyland (1968; remastered 1993). Jimi was most satisfied with this album. As the producer, Jimi was free to introduce some longer songs, including "Voodoo Chile," a 15-minute jam. This release is considered by many to be among the most significant rock albums ever recorded.

Smash Hits (1969). This album is a collection of previously released songs.

Band of Gypsys (1970; remastered 1998). A live recording made during a performance at New York's Fillmore East, this album introduces Jimi's new band. It was made to satisfy a contract dispute and was not given the same care as the previous albums.

Radio One (1988). This is a collection of live studio tracks made by the original JHE in 1967 for radio broadcast. In 1998, MCA released the live radio broadcasts remastered as a 37-track double CD, called *The BBC Sessions*.

First Rays of the New Rising Sun (1997). Released by the Hendrix family, this is meant to represent the work that Jimi did in 1968 and 1969 before he died. It includes all ten tracks of *The Cry of Love* album, which Eddie Kramer and Mitch Mitchell reworked for release in 1971.

Selected Bibliography

Brooks, Tilford. *America's Black Musical Heritage.* Englewood Cliffs, NJ: Prentice-Hall, 1984.

Chase, Gilbert. *America's Music: From the Pilgrims to the Present.* 3rd ed. Chicago: University of Chicago Press, 1987.

Glebbeek, Caesar and Douglas J. Noble. *Jimi Hendrix: The Man, the Music, the Memorabilia.* New York: Thunder's Mouth, 1996.

Guitar Player Magazine. *Guitar Player Book,* 3rd ed. New York: Grove Press, 1983.

Halliburton, Warren J. *Harlem: A History of Broken Dreams.* New York: Doubleday, 1974.

Haskins, Jim. *The Cotton Club.* New York: Random House, 1977.

Henderson, David. *'Scuse Me While I Kiss the Sky: The Life of Jimi Hendrix.* New York: Bantam, 1983, 1996.

Kozinn, Allan, et al. *The Guitar: The History, the Music, the Players.* New York: Morrow, 1984.

McDermott, John. With Billy Cox and Eddie Kramer. *Jimi Hendrix: Sessions.* Boston: Little, Brown, 1995.

McDermott, John. With Eddie Kramer. *Hendrix: Setting the Record Straight.* New York: Warner, 1993.

Miller, Jim, ed. *The Rolling Stone Illustrated History of Rock & Roll.* New York: Random House, 1980.

Mitchell, Mitch. *Jimi Hendrix: Inside the Experience.* New York: St. Martin's, 1990.

Murray, Charles Shaar. *Crosstown Traffic.* New York: St. Martin's Press, 1990.

Piccoli, Sean. *Jimi Hendrix.* Philadelphia: Chelsea House, 1997.

Potash, Chris. *The Jimi Hendrix Companion: Three Decades of Commentary.* New York: Simon & Schuster, 1996.

Redding, Noel, and Carol Appleby. *Are You Experienced?* New York: DaCapo Press, 1996.

Romanowski, Patricia, ed. *The New Rolling Stone Encyclopedia of Rock & Roll.* New York: Rolling Stone Press, 1995.

Shapiro, Harry, and Caesar Glebbeek. *Electric Gypsy.* New York: St. Martin's Press, 1995.

Welch, Chris. *Hendrix: A Biography.* New York: Quick Fox, 1978.

VIDEOS

A Film about Jimi Hendrix. Los Angeles: Warner Bros., 1973

Rock & Roll, Volume 2, Shakespeares in the Alley. Boston: WGBH Educational Foundation and the BBC, 1995.

Rock & Roll, Volume 3, Crossroads: Blues in Technicolor. Boston: WGBH Educational Foundation and the BBC, 1995.

Rock & Roll, Volume 4, Plugging In. Boston: WGBH Educational Foundation and the BBC, 1995.

Sachnoff, Marc J. *The History of Rock N' Roll–Guitar Heroes.* New York: Time-Life, 1995.

Woodstock, I & II. Michael Wadleigh, Director, 1970.

MAGAZINES & NEWSPAPER ARTICLES

Fricke, D. "Jimi: The Man and the Music." *Rolling Stone,* February 6, 1992, 40.

Jet Magazine. "Jimi Hendrix's Father Wins Control of Late Rocker's Musical Legacy," *Jet,* August 14, 1995, 24.

Johnston, Richard. "Music Was Our Lives." *Guitar Player,* August 1997, 87.

Moore, Roger. "Blunder Years," *Scene Magazine, Idaho Statesman,* August 13, 1999, 4.

Websites

Barnes, Ltd.. "1969 Woodstock Festival & Concert." *Woodstock 69* (1999). http://www.woodstock69.com/wsrprnt8.htm (September 10, 1999)

Classic Rock News. "Hendrix's Electric Ladylands [sic] Studios Partially Demolished." *Classic Rock News.* http://www.classicrock.about.com/entertainment/music/classicrock/bln0625.htm?COB=home&terms=Electric+Lady+Studios&PM=113_300_T (October 13, 1999)

Henke, James. "The Psychedelic Era 1965–1969." *Rock & Roll Hall of Fame and Museum.* http://www.rockhall.com/exhibits/featured/psychedelic.html (August 30, 1999)

Rockmine Archives. "Jimi's Death Certificate." *Jimi Hendrix.* http://www.rockmine.music.co.uk/Jimi.html (August 30, 1999)

Stockdale, Tom. *Jimi Hendrix.* Philadelphia: Chelsea House, 1998.

Univibes International Jimi Hendrix Magazine. "Photos." *Electric Lady Studios.* http://www.univibes.com (October 6, 1999)

Wilson, D. B. and Alroy. "Jimi Hendrix." *Wilson & Alroy's Record Review.* http://home.dti.net/warr/hendrix.html (August 20, 1999)

Wilson, D.B & Alroy. "60s Rock Overview." *Wilson & Alroy's Record Review.* http://home.dti.net/warr/overview.html (August 20, 1999))

Further Reading and Websites

Asivatham, Sandhya. *The History of Jazz.* New York: Chelsea House Publications, 2003.

Dell, Pamela. *The Blues: Birth of an American Sound.* Chanhassen, MN: Child's World, 2005.

Finlayson, Reggie. *We Shall Overcome: The History of the American Civil Rights Movement.* Minneapolis: Lerner Publications Company, 2003.

Kallen, Stuart A. *The History of Rock and Roll.* San Diego: Lucent Books, 2002.

Krull, Kathleen. *The Book of Rock Stars: 24 Musical Icons That Shine through History.* New York: Hyperion Press, 2003.

Medearis, Angela Shelf, and Michael R. Medearis. *Music.* New York: Henry Holt, 1997.

Official Jimi Hendrix Website
http://www.jimihendrix.com
The Official Jimi Hendrix website contains the biographical information, recent news, an online store, discography, and links to the Jimi Hendrix memorial. The site also announces the latest news on Jimi Hendrix tribute concerts and much more.

Phillips, Jane. *LSD, PCP, & Other Hallucinogens.* New York: Chelsea House, 2000.

Roberts, Jeremy. *The Beatles.* Minneapolis: Lerner Publications Company, 2002.

Roberts, Jeremy. *Bob Dylan: Voice of a Generation.* Minneapolis: Lerner Publications Company, 2005.

Rock and Roll Hall of Fame
http://www.rockhall.com
The official website of the Rock and Roll Hall of Fame Museum in Cleveland, Ohio. This website includes information on all Rock and Roll Hall of Fame members and also has links to the museum's current exhibitions.

INDEX

Photo Acknowledgments

The images in this book are used with the permission of: Museum of History and Industry, Seattle, pp. 7, 69, 70; Classmates.com Yearbook Archives, pp. 11, 15; Library of Congress, p. 17 (HABS-TENN, 19-NASH, 20-4); The Everett Collection, p. 19; © Bettmann/CORBIS, pp. 23, 96; © Hulton-Deutsch Collection/CORBIS, pp. 25, 62; © Sam Lund/Independent Picture Service (IPS), p. 26; © American Stock/Getty Images, p. 28; © Jason Lauré, pp. 31, 81, 84; © Evening Standard/Getty Images, p. 32; © Camera Press/Retna Ltd., p. 34; Tony Brown Collection, p. 35; © Michael Webb/ Hulton|Archive, Getty Images, p. 37; Retna Ltd., p. 38; © London Features International (USA) Ltd., pp. 44, 46, 67; © Platt Collection/Archive Photos/Getty Images, p. 48; © Nick Hale/Hulton|Archive/Getty Images, p. 54; © Harry Goodwin/Star File Inc., p. 57; © John Olson/ Time Life Pictures/Getty Images, p. 58; © Henry Diltz/CORBIS, p. 59; © Chris Walter, pp. 64, 98; © Popperfoto.com, p. 72; © Holland/ Retna Ltd., pp. 75, 91; © Jeff Mayer/Star File Inc., p. 79; © Ted Kessel/Globe Photos, Inc., p. 80; © Blank Archives/Getty Images, p. 85; © Photofest, p. 87; © Jim Cummins/Star File Inc., p. 88; © Neal Preston/CORBIS, p. 95; © AP/Wide World Photos, p. 100.

Front Cover: © Reuters/CORBIS